Original title:
The Map to Mutual Understanding

Copyright © 2024 Swan Charm
All rights reserved.

Author: Aron Pilviste
ISBN HARDBACK: 978-9916-86-659-7
ISBN PAPERBACK: 978-9916-86-660-3
ISBN EBOOK: 978-9916-86-661-0

A Voyage of Shared Narratives

We sail on waves of stories told,
With laughter woven, threads of gold.
Together we craft the tales we share,
In every word, a breeze of care.

From distant shores, whispers arise,
In dreams we sail beneath the skies.
Each heartbeat echoes, a guiding star,
Navigating paths both near and far.

Through storms of doubt, we find our way,
United voices, come what may.
Each narrative, a lantern bright,
Illuminating the darkest night.

In silence, bonds of trust are formed,
As tides of change become transformed.
With every tale, a bridge we build,
In the currents of life, our hearts fulfilled.

So let us gather, friends of the sea,
In this voyage of shared narrative glee.
Through laughter and tears, we'll journey on,
Together we rise with each new dawn.

Bridges Beyond Borders

Across the rivers, dreams take flight,
Building bridges in the night.
Hearts connect through whispered tales,
Uniting souls where hope prevails.

From mountain high to valley low,
Together we watch the seasons flow.
In every language, love is heard,
A bond unbroken, softly stirred.

Coordinates of Care

In every corner, kindness flows,
Wherever one may choose to go.
With every gesture, hearts align,
Mapping paths to the divine.

Along the lines of sacrifice,
Embracing warmth, we pay the price.
With open arms, we lend a hand,
Creating hope across the land.

Trails of Empathy

Winding paths through fields of grace,
Every step, a sacred space.
In silence shared, our hearts will meet,
Finding solace, bittersweet.

With a listening ear, we gather near,
Showing strength when faced with fear.
Together, we navigate the pain,
Transforming loss into the gain.

Between the Lines of Us

In subtle words, our stories lie,
Ink and hope that never die.
Between the lines, we breathe and sway,
Building trust in our own way.

A tapestry of laughter shared,
Where love blooms in form declared.
In shadows cast and light embraced,
Together, our journeys are traced.

The Compass of Connection

In the depths of silence, we find,
Hearts aligned, souls intertwined.
Mapping the stars, we trace the night,
Guided by love, our spirits take flight.

Paths cross gently, like whispers shared,
Each moment treasured, each glance declared.
Through winding roads, we learn to see,
The compass of connection, you and me.

Finding Our Bearings

Lost in the chaos, we pause to breathe,
Anchors of trust in what we believe.
With each step forward, clarity grows,
Finding our bearings where compassion flows.

The winds may shift, the tides may change,
Yet through it all, our hearts rearrange.
Together we weather the storms of doubt,
Finding our way as we figure it out.

Threads of Intimacy

Woven with care, our stories unfold,
Threads of intimacy, gentle yet bold.
In laughter and tears, the fabric we weave,
A tapestry rich with what we believe.

With every shared moment, bonds grow strong,
In whispers and secrets, where we belong.
The colors of trust paint our days bright,
Threads of intimacy, our hearts take flight.

A Network of Nuance

In small gestures, we find our way,
A network of nuance in what we say.
The subtleties linger, like soft morning light,
Guiding our feelings, igniting the night.

With every emotion, layers unfold,
A rich tapestry of stories told.
In every connection, we truly belong,
A network of nuance, we grow ever strong.

The Road of Revelations

Each step unveils hidden sights,
Truth blooms in the morning light.
Whispers of wisdom echo near,
Guiding hearts through hope and fear.

Twists and turns, the mind aligns,
With every choice, the spirit shines.
Lessons learned from journeys past,
In every shadow, courage cast.

A bridge of thoughts between the souls,
Binding stories as the heart enrolls.
With open eyes, embrace each sign,
The road reveals the truth divine.

Crossing Divide by Dialogue

In silence, walls begin to rise,
But words can mend and open ties.
With gentle tones and patient hearts,
We weave connections, play our parts.

Conversations bridge the space,
Creating warmth in shared embrace.
Through every doubt and fear we tread,
The path transforms with what is said.

Threads of understanding grow,
As empathy begins to flow.
Together we can cross the line,
And find the common heart, divine.

Tides of Trust

Like waves that crash and softly recede,
Trust flows to nurture every need.
In moments shared, we find our way,
The ebb and flow of night and day.

Anchored deep in love's embrace,
We rise together, face to face.
Through storms and calm, we hold the line,
In tides of trust, our hearts entwine.

Each promise made, a lighthouse beam,
Guiding us through every dream.
With open hearts, we weather all,
Together strong, we shall not fall.

Mending Fractured Paths

In broken roads, we search for light,
Each crack a tale of fear and fight.
Yet hands can heal what's torn apart,
With love's embrace, we make a start.

Forgiveness flows like gentle streams,
Restoring hope, rekindling dreams.
Through shattered glass, we find a way,
To piece the past and seize the day.

Guide me gently, as we tread,
On paths of peace where angels led.
Together we'll refine each scar,
And dance in sync beneath the stars.

Landscapes of Love

In valleys where soft whispers play,
Beneath the golden sun's warm ray.
The rivers of our hearts will flow,
In each embrace, our love will grow.

Mountains high, we trek in dreams,
Through forests thick, where sunlight beams.
A canvas painted with our sighs,
In every glance, our spirits rise.

The ocean's waves, they crash and call,
In twilight's glow, we risk our fall.
Together bound, we sail the tides,
In every storm, our love abides.

From meadows wide to skies so blue,
Each landscape tells a tale of you.
In every hue, our souls unite,
Together, we shine through the night.

In quiet moments shared and dear,
In laughter's song, we hold what's near.
A tapestry of lives entwined,
In love's embrace, forever blind.

Routes of Reflection

Through winding paths, we lose our way,
In silence deep, thoughts often sway.
With every step, the echoes sigh,
A mirror held to reason why.

The forest speaks through rustling leaves,
On gentle trails, the heart believes.
Each bend reveals a hidden truth,
In nature's arms, we find our youth.

Mountain peaks like dreams reside,
A journey vast with time as guide.
We re-examine all we've done,
In every shadow, find the sun.

Reflection pools beneath the stars,
Call out to us from near and far.
In quiet hours, we seek the light,
A path made clear by moon's soft sight.

As dawn awakens hopes anew,
We travel forth with courage true.
The roads we take, in trust we walk,
In every breath, our spirits talk.

Mapping Moments of Meaning

A compass held in trembling hands,
Guides through life's uncharted lands.
With every mark, a story told,
Of dreams forgotten and hopes bold.

The ticking clock draws close each phase,
In fleeting time, we carve our ways.
From laughter shared to tears that flow,
A map of moments we all know.

Through tangled threads of fate we weave,
In every joy, we learn to grieve.
A tapestry of highs and lows,
In every thread, a memory grows.

With every step, the pages turn,
In lessons learned, our spirits yearn.
Each moment framed in love and grace,
In fleeting time, we find our place.

So let us trace with open hearts,
The countless paths where meaning starts.
In every beat, a life's refrain,
Mapping moments, we lose the pain.

A Voyage of Insight

Upon the seas of thought we sail,
With open minds, we will not bail.
Each wave a lesson, bold and grand,
In search of truth, we take a stand.

The winds of change whisper and tease,
In quiet moments, we find our ease.
Through storms of doubt, we bravely ride,
With every challenge, insights hide.

The horizon gleams with dreams untold,
In every sunrise, courage bold.
As stars align, our paths will cross,
In every win, we learn from loss.

So let us navigate through time,
With hearts alight, in hope we climb.
To chart the stars, to find our way,
In the depths of night, we seize the day.

This voyage, rich in every phase,
Teaches us to cherish days.
As vessels fill with knowledge bright,
We journey forth, embracing light.

Cartography of Compassion

In the map of hearts we find,
The roads less traveled, intertwined.
Every tear, a charted stream,
Every smile, a bridge, it seems.

With ink of kindness, lines are drawn,
Creating paths from dusk till dawn.
In every shadow, light will sway,
A guiding force to lead the way.

Compasses forged in empathy,
Charting routes for you and me.
Each step forward, tender touch,
Reminds us that we care so much.

A language speaks without a word,
In silence, understanding stirred.
The borders fade, we're not alone,
In compassion's map, we've found a home.

So let's traverse this landscape wide,
With open hearts, and arms flung wide.
Together we'll explore each coast,
In cartography, we'll find our host.

Journeys Through Different Eyes

Through windows wide, the world unfolds,
In stories fresh and voices bold.
Each gaze reflects a different scheme,
A tapestry of life's grand theme.

As footsteps echo on the street,
We share a rhythm, soft and sweet.
In whispers shared, our truths arise,
A journey seen through different eyes.

In every smile, a tale is spun,
Of valleys low and mountains run.
We stand together, hand in hand,
In unity, we understand.

A landscape painted with our dreams,
Each color bright, or so it seems.
As seasons shift, perspectives change,
In every heart, a world arranged.

So let us walk on this infused land,
With visions clear, and hearts so grand.
Through journeys shared, our spirits soar,
In different eyes, we find much more.

Compass of Common Ground

In the stillness, we can find,
A compass pointing, hearts aligned.
With every heartbeat, shared and true,
We gather strength from me and you.

Through paths five-laned, we walk as one,
In shadows fallen, or warming sun.
A circle drawn with arms extended,
In common ground, we are commended.

Diverse the voices, strong their sound,
Together here, our dreams unbound.
In every struggle, hands unite,
Creating sparks that ignite the light.

As stories weave a fabric bold,
In threads of silver, blue, and gold.
Each common dream, a shared design,
A map unfolding, hearts enshrined.

In bridges built on trust and care,
Our whispered hopes dance in the air.
Let's chart the course, let love resound,
With every heartbeat, common ground.

Uncharted Territories of Dialogue

In silence broken, words take flight,
Exploring realms of day and night.
Each voice a beacon, shining bright,
In uncharted lands, we find the light.

Through twists and turns, we craft our speech,
In open hearts, new paths we reach.
No boundaries hold what thoughts ignite,
In dialogue, we find our right.

With questions posed and courage shown,
We build the soil where seeds are sown.
In fertile ground, new dreams are born,
From every challenge, we are sworn.

A tapestry of talk we weave,
In honesty, we shall believe.
Through every difference, we transcend,
In uncharted lands, new bonds we mend.

As journeys guide us, hand in hand,
With open minds, we'll understand.
In dialogues deep, we find our way,
In territories new, we'll choose to stay.

Navigating Through Differences

In stormy seas, we find our way,
With charts of heart, we choose to stay.
Voices rise, then soft they fall,
Together we stand, together we call.

Across the waves, our stories blend,
Each current's pull, a message we send.
Different shores, yet hand in hand,
Creating bridges, a steadfast band.

In colors bright, our truths unfold,
Each map a tale, each tale bold.
Navigating through the vast unknown,
In every heartbeat, we've grown.

Stars above, like dreams in flight,
Guide us through the darkest night.
With every breath, we seek to vow,
To honor the self, and honor the now.

Through differences, we find our lanes,
In harmony, we break the chains.
With open hearts, we choose to roam,
In this shared voyage, we find our home.

The Voyage of Vulnerability

Set sail on waves of hidden fears,
The compass points to open tears.
In tender winds, our spirits soar,
Embracing the depths, we yearn for more.

With every swell, we must decide,
To anchor deep or with the tides glide.
In fragile moments, strength does rise,
Finding courage in soft goodbyes.

Unraveled maps, our hearts laid bare,
In shared silence, we find the air.
Vulnerability, a beacon bright,
Guiding us through the endless night.

Through storms of doubt and waves of pain,
We forge our path, we break the chain.
Connected souls, we sail as one,
Each instance of trust—a journey begun.

And when the sun breaks through the haze,
We bask in warmth of shared praise.
In the voyage of hearts, we find our way,
Together, we rise, come what may.

Uniting the Mapmakers

Gather around, all dreamers and sparks,
Each line of our maps tells tales of arcs.
With ink and hope, we sketch our way,
Uniting voices in bright display.

Crafting dreams, we shape the land,
Each alteration, a guiding hand.
Boundaries blurred, horizons wide,
In kinship found, there's nothing to hide.

With laughter soft, and visions bold,
We weave our threads of stories untold.
Together we rise, the winds our guide,
In unity found, our dreams collide.

From every corner, our colors blend,
Charting the course, with love we send.
Through hills and valleys, together we roam,
In unity of spirit, we've found our home.

As mapmakers strong, we stand side by side,
In each gentle stroke, our hearts abide.
Drawing paths of connection, hand in hand,
Creating a future, together we stand.

Cartographers of Care

In quiet moments, our hearts align,
Mapping the places where we shine.
Through valleys deep and mountains high,
We gather strength, we learn to fly.

With every stroke, care guides the pen,
Drawing a world where love begins again.
Our charts reveal the beauty inside,
In every crease, our spirits reside.

Through trials faced, and paths yet bare,
We navigate journeys, as cartographers of care.
Hand in hand, we'll share the weight,
Creating a bond, it's never too late.

In every tear, a map unfolds,
Teaching us warmth, as each truth holds.
With every touch, a promise made,
To tend to the hearts, never to fade.

As cartographers, we write our tale,
In moments shared, we will prevail.
Through depths of compassion, we'll chart the skies,
Guiding each other, we'll rise and rise.

The Road Less Traveled

In whispers soft, the journey calls,
Two paths diverge beneath the palls.
Step forth in faith, the brave shall roam,
The heart's own path, a place called home.

The trail is wild, with thorns and blooms,
Each twist unveils fresh scents and hues.
With keenest eyes, the seeker sees,
What lies beneath the whispered trees.

With every choice, the soul grows wise,
In quiet steps, our truth belies.
The road ahead, though steep and long,
Will guide you where your heart belongs.

Signposts of Shared Sentiment

In glances soft, a bond is forged,
Each heart a canvas, bright and gorged.
With words unspoken, feelings bloom,
Together we dance, dispelling gloom.

A smile exchanged, the world ignites,
A flicker of hope on starry nights.
Through trials faced, we hold on tight,
In shared sentiment, we find our light.

The signs we pass, both clear and vague,
Reflect the tales that hearts still wage.
In every glance, a vivid thread,
We weave together, fears shed.

Guiding Stars of Interconnection

Above us shine, the stars aligned,
In constellations, we're entwined.
With every gaze into the sky,
We feel the ties that never die.

Each story told, a guiding spark,
In the vast night, we leave our mark.
Through storms and calm, they light the way,
Connected souls, come what may.

In echoes deep, our voices blend,
A harmony that knows no end.
Through darkened hours, we unite,
In guiding stars, we find our light.

Landscapes of Listening

In silence deep, the world unfolds,
The whispers soft, the heart beholds.
With open ears, the mind can roam,
In landscapes vast, we find our home.

Each story shared, a thread of grace,
In listening, we find our place.
The hills of trust, the valleys wide,
In every heart, our hopes confide.

Beneath the surface, wisdom flows,
In shared silence, compassion grows.
In quiet spaces, souls can bloom,
In landscapes of listening, there's room.

Footprints in the Sand of Time

Footprints washed away by tide,
Memories linger, never hide.
Each step echoes, soft and clear,
In the sands, I feel you near.

Waves of time, they ebb and flow,
Carrying whispers we both know.
With every grain, a story told,
In fleeting moments, love unfolds.

Beneath the sun, beneath the stars,
Every journey leaves its scars.
Yet in the vastness, we shall find,
Endless footprints left behind.

In twilight's glow, shadows play,
Guardians of the words we say.
Together still, we walk anew,
Through the sands, just me and you.

Like tides that turn, our paths align,
In the canvas of design.
Though moments fade and time may bend,
Your footprints with me never end.

The Intersection of Souls

In the garden where hearts meet,
Souls converge in rhythmic beat.
Threads entwined, a tapestry,
Woven deep in mystery.

Eyes that speak without a sound,
In silence, sacred truths are found.
Through the noise, we find our song,
A harmony where we belong.

Paths that crossed, the stars aligned,
In every glance, a love defined.
Moments fleeting, yet profound,
In the intersection, we're unbound.

Dancing lightly on this stage,
A chapter written, turn the page.
With each heartbeat, I embrace,
The beautiful, timeless grace.

Though distance may attempt to tear,
Invisible threads still bind us there.
We are forever intertwined,
Two souls one journey, love divine.

A Journey to Kindred Spirits

Through valleys deep and mountains high,
We seek the truth beneath the sky.
On this path where dreams ignite,
Kindred spirits shine so bright.

With every step, a story grows,
In whispered winds, the universe knows.
Together we navigate the dark,
Finding warmth in every spark.

Laughter echoes, tears may flow,
In the garden, seeds we sow.
Hand in hand, we face the night,
Chasing shadows, finding light.

In unity, we forge a bond,
Through every wave, of life we're fond.
With hearts as one, we chart the course,
In love and trust, our guiding force.

This journey shared, a sacred art,
In every ending, a brand new start.
Each moment cherished, spirits soar,
In kindred love, forevermore.

Charting the Unseen

In the silence, secrets lay,
Mapping worlds where dreamers play.
With every thought, a canvas bright,
We chart the unseen, find the light.

Through the shadows, visions bloom,
In whispered hopes, dispelling gloom.
Colors dance, the soul ignites,
As we wander through endless nights.

Questions linger, answers hide,
Yet in our hearts, dreams reside.
With open minds, we too shall see,
The beauty of what's yet to be.

Stars above paint stories bold,
In galaxies, our hearts unfold.
With every leap into the unknown,
We find a place we can call home.

Together, we embrace the vast,
In a tapestry, woven fast.
For in the unseen, truth is found,
And love, unbound, forever crowned.

Embracing Our Differences

In colors bright, we stand together,
Each story told, a thread of tether.
What makes us unique, a vibrant song,
In harmony, we all belong.

Different paths that weave and wind,
In every soul, new truths we find.
Through open hearts, we share our light,
Transforming shadows into sight.

The beauty lies in every shade,
In every choice, the risks we've made.
With hands entwined, we break the mold,
In unity, our strength unfolds.

Celebrate the ways we vary,
In every laugh, in every worry.
Together we rise, never apart,
Embracing the world, the human heart.

Horizons of Hope

Beneath the sky, dreams start to soar,
With every sunrise, we seek for more.
Stars guide us on this winding way,
Leading us gently through night and day.

Fields of gold, where wishes bloom,
In whispered winds, we cast away gloom.
With every step and every chance,
We dance anew in life's sweet trance.

Mountains high call out our names,
Through trials faced, we fan the flames.
In unity, our hearts ignite,
Together strong, we find the light.

The future's bright, a canvas unspun,
With colors bold, we've just begun.
In every shadow, hope will rise,
A tapestry woven under skies.

Conversations in the Wilderness

In forests deep, where secrets lie,
We gather 'round, with hearts open wide.
Whispers of nature guide our quest,
In shared silence, we find our rest.

Every rustle, a story told,
Through branches swaying, courage bold.
Amongst the trees, we seek the truth,
In every moment, reclaim our youth.

Beneath the stars, we dream and speak,
In solitude, it's connection we seek.
Voices blend with the night's soft sigh,
In wilderness, our spirits fly.

Through rivers flowing, and mountains wide,
We carry peace, where love resides.
In nature's arms, we find our way,
In conversations, we long to stay.

The Confluence of Hearts

Two rivers flow, entwined in grace,
In every glance, a warm embrace.
Together we merge, no end in sight,
In love's sweet dance, the world feels right.

With every heartbeat, stories blend,
In every moment, we transcend.
The rhythm of us, a tender song,
In this confluence, we belong.

Laughter echoes through valleys deep,
In shared joys, our promises keep.
Through storms we weather, hand in hand,
In unity, our dreams expand.

As seasons change, our roots grow strong,
In the garden of life, we belong.
Each heartbeat fuels the fire within,
In the confluence where love begins.

Fables of Fertile Ground

In fields where dreams take flight,
Seeds whisper soft and bright.
The sunbeams dance with grace,
Nurturing each hidden place.

From roots, the tales arise,
Beneath the endless skies.
Every leaf tells a story,
Of life, of love, of glory.

With every raindrop's kiss,
Fables bloom, a tender bliss.
In harmony, they grow,
Painting the earth's vibrant show.

Time winds like a gentle stream,
Carving out each hopeful dream.
In fertile ground, they stand tall,
Together, they will not fall.

Through seasons' grace and shift,
Nature's hands, a timeless gift.
In our hearts, these tales remain,
Echoing beyond the plain.

The Journey of Joint Sentiments

Two hearts embark as one,
Underneath the golden sun.
Each step a shared delight,
Guided by love's radiant light.

Through valleys lush and wide,
In each other, they confide.
Hand in hand, they explore,
Opening every door.

In laughter's warm embrace,
They find their sacred space.
While shadows may appear,
Their bond will persevere.

With dreams woven in trust,
They rise from any dust.
Together, they ignite,
A timeless, brilliant light.

Each memory they weave,
In love, they still believe.
The journey, rich and bold,
In their hearts, the story unfolds.

A Tidal Wave of Understanding

Waves crash upon the shore,
Whispers of what came before.
In depth, the ocean sighs,
Secrets hidden, where truth lies.

Through currents strong and deep,
We dive into what we keep.
Every tide, a new embrace,
An ocean filled with grace.

Understanding flows like streams,
Catching us in gentle dreams.
The depths of hearts align,
A dance of souls entwined.

In storms, we find our way,
Guided by the light of day.
Each wave, a lesson learned,
With every turn, we are turned.

Together, we shall stand,
Drifting on this endless sand.
A tidal wave to bind,
In harmony, we find.

Crossroads of Kindred Spirits

At twilight's gentle call,
Two paths converge, they stall.
In silence, they will meet,
Where kindred souls greet.

The air is thick with fate,
In this moment, they wait.
Stories shared in glances,
Life's rhythm, it enhances.

Each choice may branch anew,
Their bond will guide them through.
In laughter and in tears,
They conquer all their fears.

With hearts open wide,
They'll walk side by side.
Every step, a journey bold,
In their truth, they unfold.

Together, they create,
A tapestry of fate.
At the crossroads, they find,
A love that's intertwined.

Seeking Common Ground

In fields where hearts collide,
We find our pathways blend,
With open minds and arms,
Together we can mend.

Beneath the sky so wide,
We share our hopes and dreams,
Through laughter, tears, and time,
We weave our silent schemes.

Each difference a thread,
A tapestry of light,
In unity we stand,
And face the coming night.

With kindness as our guide,
We seek the shared embrace,
In every heart we touch,
We find our common space.

Let voices echo clear,
In harmony's sweet sound,
For when we walk as one,
We've truly found our ground.

Guiding Stars of Understanding

In darkness we can find,
A beacon shining bright,
With every star aligned,
We share our guiding light.

For in the vast unknown,
We look to one another,
Our stories intertwined,
As sister, friend, or brother.

Through storms and gentle nights,
We navigate the seas,
With trust as our compass,
We sail with heartfelt ease.

The map of human souls,
Is rich with every tale,
In empathy's embrace,
We learn to gently sail.

Together we ascend,
To heights we've never seen,
With stars of understanding,
We live the shared dream.

Compass Rose of Relationship

In circles we explore,
The paths that twist and turn,
With every step we take,
New truths for us to learn.

A compass set on trust,
Leads us to deeper seas,
Where love becomes the map,
And hope carries the breeze.

Through seasons we will grow,
With courage and with grace,
In every heart we share,
We find our rightful place.

With laughter as our guide,
And patience in our sails,
We navigate the waves,
And weave our tender tales.

Let's chart a course of joy,
In every rise and fall,
Together we will find,
We have it all, through all.

Unveiling Shared Stories

With every word we speak,
A story comes to life,
In whispers of the past,
We find the joy and strife.

As layers peel away,
The truth begins to shine,
In every tale retold,
We weave the hearts in line.

In moments fiercely bright,
Or shadows we conceal,
We gather 'round the fire,
And share what's truly real.

With open hearts we stand,
In the circle of exchange,
Our laughter binds the thread,
As worlds begin to change.

So let the stories flow,
Like rivers deep and wide,
For in our shared narratives,
The strongest bonds abide.

Exploring the Terrain of Tolerance

In fields where kindness grows wide,
We walk together, side by side.
With hearts open, we'll share the space,
To nurture peace, our common grace.

Each difference, a color so bright,
A canvas painted with pure light.
Through valleys deep and mountains tall,
We'll find our strength, together we stand tall.

Paths may twist, and shadows fall,
Yet, in each heart, we can hear the call.
With patience we'll climb every hill,
Creating a bridge with unwavering will.

In silence, respect is deeply sown,
In laughter, a bond is beautifully grown.
The terrain we travel is vast indeed,
Together we flourish, together we lead.

Footprints in the Sand of Understanding

Each step we take leaves a mark,
In the sand where dreams embark.
With every wave, a story unfolds,
Of hearts uniting, brave and bold.

The sun sets low, painting skies bright,
Reminding us of shared delight.
Hand in hand, we tread the shore,
With each moment, we yearn for more.

The tides may shift, the winds may change,
Yet our bond will never estrange.
In whispers of waves, we find our way,
Together, we'll face each new day.

Through bursts of laughter and moments of tears,
We navigate through hopes and fears.
With every footprint, a promise we make,
In the sand of life, together we wake.

A Voyage in Unity

Set sail on a sea of dreams,
With open hearts, we find our themes.
The stars above guide our way,
Together in unity, come what may.

The currents may twist, the storms might roar,
Yet hand in hand, we'll explore.
Each wave a tale, each breeze a song,
In the journey together, we all belong.

The horizon brings new sights to see,
In every face, a memory.
With sails unfurled, our spirits soar,
Across the waters, we'll forever explore.

Anchors of trust hold us tight,
In the depths of the night's soft light.
Together we brave the vast unknown,
In the voyage of unity, love is shown.

Coordinates of Kindness

In a world mapped by hearts so bright,
We trace each line with pure delight.
Coordinates set in love's embrace,
Guiding us to every sacred space.

With every gesture, kindness ignites,
A ripple that dances, soaring heights.
From one soul to another, it flows,
In this garden of grace, compassion grows.

The notes of laughter, a sweet refrain,
Echo the beauty found in the rain.
Together we wander through valleys wide,
Each step a promise, hearts open wide.

Maps may differ, yet we align,
In the compass of love, our paths entwine.
Coordinates of kindness, so profound,
In every heartbeat, true joy is found.

Points of Harmony

In the stillness of the night,
Whispers dance, soft and bright.
Hearts align like stars on high,
Embracing dreams that gently sigh.

Notes of laughter fill the air,
Woven threads of joy to share.
In every glance, a spark ignites,
Guiding souls through endless flights.

Hands entwined in silent grace,
Finding solace in this space.
With every beat, a rhythm flows,
Unfolding love that only grows.

Beneath the sun's warm, golden glow,
Friendship blossoms, hearts in tow.
In moments small, the world aligns,
Creating life where beauty shines.

Through trials faced, we stand as one,
Chasing dreams 'til day is done.
In unity, we find our way,
Points of harmony at play.

Atlas of Affection

Maps of kindness drawn in lines,
Every crease a love that shines.
In every corner, hearts hold tight,
Guiding us through darkest night.

With every touch, a story told,
In warmth and care, we find our gold.
Through oceans vast, our spirits soar,
An atlas made of hearts we adore.

Each moment shared, a precious thread,
In laughter's glow, we forge ahead.
Through valleys deep, our voices blend,
An endless journey with no end.

Through fleeting time, our love will last,
Building bridges from the past.
In every heartbeat, trust grows wide,
In this atlas, we confide.

With tender maps our souls explore,
In every hug, we seek for more.
Holding close the dreams we weave,
In this affection, we believe.

Echoes of Togetherness

In quiet moments, echoes ring,
Whispered thoughts on gentle wing.
Together bound, we share our souls,
In every beat, connection rolls.

Through sunsets kissed by golden rays,
We find our strength in shared arrays.
In laughter's song and silence true,
The echoes sing of me and you.

In paths we tread, both new and old,
The stories shared, a treasure bold.
In tears and smiles, we hold the line,
Echoes of a love divine.

Through tangled roots, our bond remains,
In every joy, in every pain.
As seasons change, we stand as one,
Together bright like morning sun.

Through every chapter, hand in hand,
In echoes soft, we understand.
United by the love we share,
Together always, ever rare.

The Journey of Listening

In quiet spaces, stories unfold,
In gentle whispers, truths are told.
With eager hearts, we lean in close,
The journey blooms, the spirit grows.

As kindness flows, we learn to hear,
Each voice a melody, bright and clear.
In silence shared, we find our way,
The journey of listening, day by day.

Through winding paths and turns unseen,
With open hearts, we know what's been.
In every moment, lessons learned,
The fire of trust, forever burned.

With every heartbeat, bonds we trace,
Through words unspoken, find our place.
In every pause, a sacred space,
The journey sings of love's embrace.

From distant shores to nearby streams,
In listening, we find our dreams.
Together woven, spirits fly,
In this journey, hearts reply.

The Rhythm of Relational Discovery

In whispers shared and secrets told,
Connections bloom, like petals bold.
Each heartbeat echoes, soft and clear,
A dance of trust, drawing near.

Through laughter bright and shadows cast,
We find our way, both slow and fast.
In every glance, a story weaves,
A tapestry that never leaves.

Barefoot upon the path of chance,
We twirl and spin, lost in the dance.
With every step, our spirits play,
In harmony, we learn the way.

As seasons turn, our lives entwine,
United hearts, robust divine.
Each moment cherished, ever true,
A boundless realm, just me and you.

In silent pauses, truths unfold,
The rhythm grows, a warmth to hold.
With open arms, we brave the new,
In every beat, our love shines through.

Harvesting Hues of Humanity

In fields of thought, rich colors blend,
Voices rise, as hearts extend.
Each face a canvas, stories untold,
A tapestry of dreams unfold.

From laughter's joy to sorrow's sigh,
In every shade, we learn to fly.
With hands united, drawing near,
We cultivate the seeds of cheer.

In gentle winds, the whispers flow,
Echoing truths that softly grow.
With every heartbeat, a song we share,
A vibrant pulse, beyond compare.

Through shadows deep and sunlight's grace,
We find our roots, in time and space.
As colors merge, a vision clear,
In unity, we conquer fear.

Harvesting dreams, we sow the light,
In every heart, a spark ignites.
Together, we rise, a swirling throng,
In hues of hope, we all belong.

The Symphony of Synchronized Souls

In perfect harmony, we breathe,
A melody of trust we weave.
With every note, our spirits soar,
In symphonic grace, we ask for more.

The rhythm pulses through our veins,
Each heartbeat cherished, no more chains.
Together, we explore the vast,
In every echo, shadows cast.

With instruments of love, we play,
In unity, we light the way.
Each voice a thread, entwined and strong,
A chorus rich where we belong.

As crescendos rise to touch the stars,
We cast away our hidden scars.
Through symphonies, our souls ignite,
Together we shine, a brilliant light.

In gentle moments, silence speaks,
With every glance, connection peaks.
In this grand orchestra of fate,
We find our place, and love creates.

Across the Great Divide

A chasm lies where dreams once bloomed,
But hope ignites, where hearts are groomed.
With bridges built from fervent sighs,
We cross the gap, as spirits rise.

In distant lands, the same stars shine,
Drawing us near, a sacred line.
With hands outstretched, we reach for light,
In darkness, find a spark so bright.

Though storms may rage and winds may howl,
Together, we are strong, we growl.
With every step, we break the mold,
In unity, our stories told.

In every heartbeat, echoes blend,
A song of peace, we'll always send.
Across the divide, through thick and thin,
A journey shared, let love begin.

For in each heart, a yearning dwells,
With open arms, our longing swells.
Together we'll traverse the tide,
In the end, we walk side by side.

Collective Coordinates

In the map of dreams, we chart our way,
Connections weave in the light of day.
Hearts aligned in a cosmic dance,
Together we rise, in fate's sweet chance.

Silent whispers across the night,
Echoes of hope, our guiding light.
Starlit paths on this endless quest,
Finding solace in shared unrest.

Threads of longing in a fabric sewn,
United hearts, never alone.
Each point a story, each line a song,
In every heartbeat, we all belong.

Waves of laughter, currents of tears,
Carried along by the weight of years.
Through valleys low and mountains high,
Together we soar, together we fly.

In the endless sky, our spirits blend,
Where journeys pause and moments mend.
Together we wander, forever free,
In this vast universe, you and me.

Meeting in the Middle

Two paths converge in the evening glow,
With every step, we start to know.
The space between us, a sacred trust,
In the dance of fate, we must adjust.

Moments linger like whispers sweet,
In the quiet, our hearts meet.
Understanding flows like a gentle stream,
In the stillness, we build a dream.

With hands outstretched, we bridge the gap,
In shared laughter, we begin to tap.
Each story shared a thread of gold,
In the tapestry of friendship, bold.

The world around may swirl and spin,
But here in the middle is where we begin.
A union formed in trust and grace,
Two souls united in this sacred space.

In the spectrum of colors, we find our hue,
Turning the ordinary into something new.
Together we stand, as shadows fall,
Meeting in the middle, we conquer all.

Stories Told in Shadows

In twilight's hour, secrets unfold,
Whispers of dreams, and stories told.
Shadows dance on the walls of night,
Echoes of lives once filled with light.

Flickering tales in the fading glow,
Every silhouette, a story to show.
In the quiet corners, memories play,
In the hush of dusk, they find their way.

Ghosts of laughter in the air so thin,
Past and present, where time has been.
With every shadow, the past collides,
In the heart's canvas, love abides.

Steps that linger in the silver mist,
Each moment cherished, never missed.
In the tapestry woven with threads of grace,
Shadows reveal their sacred place.

As the night deepens, the stories grow,
In every heartbeat, their wisdom flows.
Tales of yearning, of hope and fear,
In the silence, their voices are clear.

The Symphony of Similarities

In the orchestra of life, we play our part,
Notes of laughter that touch the heart.
In harmony's embrace, we find our song,
Together we weave, where we belong.

Different backgrounds, yet spirits aligned,
In the rhythm of life, the beauty we find.
Melodies blend, like colors that mix,
In this symphony, we create our fix.

Each story shared is a unique refrain,
In the vast concert, we rise again.
Layered in truth, wrapped in love,
Guided by stars that shine from above.

United we stand in our fragile grace,
Finding strength in this common space.
With every heartbeat, the tempo grows,
In the symphony of life, our essence flows.

As the final note hangs in the air,
We celebrate differences, stripped bare.
In a world of noise, let love be our guide,
In this grand symphony, we shall abide.

The Horizon of Harmony

Beneath the golden sun's embrace,
We gather in this sacred space.
Voices rise, a melody clear,
Each note a heartbeat we hold dear.

Together we weave dreams so bright,
In the warmth of shared delight.
Hand in hand, we walk this way,
Creating joy in every day.

As rivers flow, we find our course,
In unity, we find our force.
A tapestry of hopes aligned,
In every soul, a heart entwined.

The horizon calls, a vivid scene,
Where peace is born, and love is keen.
We chase the whispers on the breeze,
In harmony, we find our ease.

With every step, the dawn will rise,
A canvas painted with our ties.
Together strong, we lift the veil,
In every heart, our dreams prevail.

Skyways of Solidarity

Above the clouds, in azure skies,
We soar as one, our spirits rise.
Through winds of change, we find our way,
Together strong, we greet the day.

In every challenge, hand in hand,
We build a world, a promised land.
Voices echo, steadfast, clear,
In unity, we cast our fear.

Like stars that twinkle in the night,
Our hopes collide, a brilliant light.
Skyways stretch, horizons blend,
Solidarity, our truest friend.

With every flight, we break the chains,
Injustice falls where kindness reigns.
Together we'll rise above the storm,
In every heart, a place that's warm.

So let us dream and reach for more,
A future bright, on peace we'll soar.
In every heart, a song we share,
Skyways of hope, we breathe the air.

Constellations of Commonality

In the night sky, stars align,
Mapping paths both yours and mine.
Connected, we weave a cosmic tale,
In constellations, we will not fail.

Every twinkle, a voice so true,
Reflecting the love that lives in you.
Together we shine, a luminous sea,
Guided by light, forever free.

With every heartbeat, we remind,
In the quiet, our hopes are blind.
Diverse yet one, we draw the map,
In unity's cradle, we gently clasp.

Across the vastness, we reach out wide,
In kindness, let compassion guide.
As galaxies spin, we'll find our way,
In common dreams, we choose to stay.

Through shadows deep, we'll find our light,
In the dance of stars, we unite.
Constellations bright, our spirits call,
In every heart, we rise, we fall.

Paving the Path to Peace

With every stone, we lay the ground,
In quiet strength, our hopes abound.
Brick by brick, we build the way,
A future bright, where hearts won't sway.

Through trials faced, we grow in grace,
In every tear, we find our place.
Together we toil, hand in hand,
In trust and love, we make our stand.

When stormy skies cloud our view,
In whispered hopes, we see it through.
Paving paths where kindness flows,
In every nook, a garden grows.

With open hearts, we share our dreams,
In unity, the light redeems.
A tapestry rich, woven with care,
In every soul, a spark to share.

Let's chart the course for all to see,
In every voice, a symphony.
Paving paths, we leave our mark,
Together we rise, ignite the spark.

Discovering New Latitude

Beneath the endless sky we roam,
Into the wild, we call it home.
Each whisper guides, a compass true,
In nature's arms, we start anew.

The mountains rise, a daunting quest,
With every step, we seek the best.
Through forests deep and rivers wide,
Our hearts entwined, a sacred ride.

With every dawn, the world awakes,
In silent dreams, the journey makes.
We shed our fears, embrace the sun,
In newfound light, our souls are one.

The winds of change, they sing to me,
A symphony of mystery.
With every turn, a lesson learned,
In every leap, a passion burned.

Together we explore the stars,
With open hearts, no bounds, no bars.
In wandering paths, we find our fate,
A dance of dreams, we co-create.

Chasing Shared Visions

In twilight's glow, we cast our dreams,
With hearts ablaze, or so it seems.
A tapestry of hope we weave,
In every breath, we dare believe.

With every word, a bridge we build,
Through laughter shared, our spirits thrilled.
United paths, through thick and thin,
In every loss, a chance to win.

Through valleys low and mountains high,
We chase the stars, we dare to fly.
With every step, we grow in trust,
In faith, we rise, from earth to dust.

The echoes of our laughter ring,
In harmony, our spirits sing.
A symphony of souls combined,
In friendship's light, our hearts aligned.

Together we will face the dawn,
With every fear and doubt withdrawn.
Through storms and calm, we'll find our way,
In chasing dreams, we live each day.

The Odyssey of Insight

In search of wisdom, we embark,
With every question, we ignite a spark.
Through storms of thought, we find our course,
In realms of mind, we tap the source.

From shadows cast by doubt and fear,
To prisms bright, where truths appear.
In quietude, the answers bloom,
Transforming dark into the room.

Each journey taken leaves a trace,
In every heart, an open space.
The stars above, they seem to guide,
Through swirling thoughts, our dreams abide.

With every turn of fate and chance,
We gather strength, we learn to dance.
In every tear, a river flows,
Each insight gained, a flower grows.

Bonded by the quest we share,
In unison, we breathe the air.
In silent night, reflections shine,
In every heartbeat, truths combine.

Diverging Paths Converge

In quiet moments, paths first part,
Yet destiny can bind the heart.
Through winding roads, our truth will lead,
In every tale, the soul takes heed.

From distant shores, our journeys wend,
With dreams we chase, and hearts to mend.
The bridges built, with care and grace,
In life's embrace, we'll find our place.

Through every storm, we learn to stand,
In shadows cast, we seek the hand.
Together turned, we forge anew,
In unity, our vision grew.

As seasons change and time unfolds,
A tapestry of stories told.
From different worlds, we gather near,
In shared embrace, our purpose clear.

Though paths may twist and turn away,
In love's own light, we choose to stay.
In every step, a bond is made,
In diverging paths, the truth displayed.

The Compass of Community

In every heart, a secret song,
We gather close, where we belong.
Through joy and pain, we share the trust,
Together we rise, together we must.

Hands entwined, we shape our fate,
In unity, we create our state.
The compass spins, we find our way,
In love's embrace, we choose to stay.

Voices blend in harmony,
Painting dreams for all to see.
A tapestry of different hues,
Woven tight, with colorful views.

With each step, we light the path,
In laughter shared, we escape the wrath.
Community whispers, fierce and true,
In every struggle, we see it through.

So let the stars guide our night,
In every soul, a spark of light.
Together we rise, together we soar,
In the compass of community, forevermore.

Horizon of Understanding

As dawn breaks forth, we see the light,
With open hearts, we take our flight.
Curiosity leads the way,
To paint the world in shades of gray.

Every question opens doors,
Every answer, a chance to explore.
Beyond the veil, beyond the sound,
In the horizon, truths abound.

With every story, lessons learned,
Our minds expand as wisdom burns.
A bridge of thoughts, we build with care,
An understanding that we all can share.

Differences are merely threads,
In the fabric of our heads.
We weave a world of rich delight,
In seeking truth, we find the light.

So come, embrace the vast unknown,
In every heart, seeds are sown.
The horizon whispers, clear and bright,
A world united, in shared insight.

Bridges Built on Words

With words as stones, we pave the way,
Building bridges that will not sway.
Each sentence crafted, each line defined,
In the landscape of thoughts, we entwine.

Echoes of whispers, heard so clear,
Bridges of trust, built without fear.
Every dialogue a step we take,
In the warmth of connection, bonds awake.

Voices resonate, our spirits rise,
In shared stories, we recognize.
From silence, hope begins to bloom,
Our words dispel the shadows loom.

Conversations spark, igniting minds,
Understanding blooms, true love binds.
In every promise, we carve our fate,
Bridges of words, we celebrate.

So let us speak, let us create,
In this world, let hearts narrate.
Bridges built on words so true,
Shall lead us home, me and you.

Terrain of Openness

In fields of dreams, we roam so free,
With open hearts, we seek to see.
Mountains high and valleys low,
In the terrain of openness, we grow.

With courage as our guiding star,
We journey forth, no matter how far.
Embracing change, the winds may sway,
In every challenge, we find our way.

The landscape shifts, yet we remain,
Finding beauty in joy and pain.
Each step a choice, each turn a chance,
In the open terrain, we advance.

With every voice, a path is laid,
In mosaic hearts, our fears allayed.
Embracing differences, we learn to thrive,
In the terrain of openness, we come alive.

So let us wander, together as one,
Under the skies, beneath the sun.
In this vast landscape, rich and wide,
Openness together, our hearts abide.

The Journey of Many Roads

On paths unseen, we wander wide,
Each step we take, a shift in tide.
With every turn, our spirits soar,
A journey shared, forevermore.

Through valleys low and mountains steep,
The dreams we chase, the hopes we keep.
Guided by stars that brightly gleam,
We find our way, we chase the dream.

With laughter loud and whispers soft,
We feel the pull, we rise aloft.
In shadows cast, in daylight's glow,
The journey's heart begins to flow.

Each road we tread, a story told,
Of friendships forged and hearts of gold.
Together we face the vast unknown,
In every step, we've truly grown.

The roads may twist, but still we stand,
With open hearts and outstretched hands.
For in this journey, side by side,
We find our strength, our hopes collide.

Treading New Grounds

In fields anew, we set our sights,
With dreams afire, we chase the lights.
The path is fresh, the air is kind,
Together, new adventures find.

With every step, we break the mold,
In whispers shared, our fears unfold.
Through push and pull, we learn to grow,
On new horizons, hopes will flow.

A tapestry of vibrant hues,
We weave our fate with every muse.
As roots take hold in fertile ground,
We thrive in places yet unbound.

With courage strong, we bear the weight,
Of dreams that flourish, seeds of fate.
Though storms may come, we stand and face,
In treading new, we find our place.

Each moment rich with promise bright,
In boundless reach, we take our flight.
With hearts aflame and spirits free,
We tread new grounds, just you and me.

The Unfolding Narrative

In pages blank, our story waits,
With dreams and hopes that recreate.
Each line a thread, each twist a turn,
An unfolding tale, we yearn to learn.

With every chapter, lessons grow,
In laughter's echo and sorrow's glow.
The ink may smudge, the tale may bend,
But in each pulse, we find a friend.

Through joy and pain, the pages blend,
A narrative where hearts commend.
In shadows cast, in light so bright,
Our story shines, a guiding light.

With every voice, a truth revealed,
In vivid scenes, our fates unveiled.
The narrative, a shared embrace,
In every heart, a sacred space.

As authors bold, we write each line,
Together crafting, intertwining.
The narrative unfolds, a grand design,
In every heartbeat, our lives align.

Stories Intertwined

In woven threads, our tales combine,
The stories shared, they intertwine.
With voices rich, we speak as one,
In harmony, our lives begun.

Through laughter bright and tears we shed,
The chapters blend, the colors spread.
Each journey held in tender grace,
A tapestry time won't erase.

With open hearts, we navigate,
The paths that twist, the lines of fate.
In every glance, a tale is spun,
A bond as deep as setting sun.

The threads of life, a vibrant seam,
In shared embrace, we weave the dream.
Through trials faced and triumphs gained,
In stories intertwined, love remained.

As seasons change, we grow, we learn,
In every turn, new hopes we earn.
In this grand weave, we find the key,
That binds our stories, you and me.

Labyrinth of Perspectives

In shadows where whispers dwell,
Each twist reveals a hidden spell.
Voices echo, thoughts collide,
In the maze where truths abide.

Through winding paths, we roam and seek,
New visions rise from what we speak.
Each turn a chance to understand,
As views unite in common land.

Colors blend in twilight's grace,
Diverse stories, every face.
Together we traverse the space,
Finding peace in every place.

With every step, we shift our gaze,
Challenging life's intricate maze.
In unity, we overcome,
Learning lessons, one by one.

So let us walk, both bold and free,
In this labyrinth of harmony.
Hold out your hand, take a chance,
In the dance where all hearts prance.

The Terrain of Tolerance

Across the valleys, wide and vast,
A tapestry of futures cast.
Mountains rise, yet bridges flow,
In this land where kindness grows.

We tread on soil, rich and deep,
Learning secrets that we keep.
Step by step, beyond the line,
A heart's embrace, so pure, divine.

Grass and stones beneath our feet,
Every heartbeat feels the beat.
As differences begin to fade,
In unity, we're unafraid.

Through storms that howl and winds that wail,
Compassion's compass will not fail.
Though paths may diverge, we find,
A common goal binds all mankind.

With open arms, we greet the day,
Together we can find our way.
In the terrain of our embrace,
Tolerance blooms in every space.

Weaving Common Threads

In the loom where hearts are spun,
Threads of joy and sorrow run.
Colors bright against the gray,
Together we will find our way.

From many fibers, strong and true,
A pattern forms in every hue.
Intertwined, our stories blend,
A masterpiece around the bend.

Each stitch a tale that we hold dear,
In whispered hopes, the dreams appear.
With every knot, our lives entwined,
Creating more than we designed.

Through trials and triumph, we create,
A fabric rich with love, not hate.
In unity, our voices soar,
Woven tales that seek for more.

So let us weave with gentle hands,
Crafting bonds across all lands.
In the tapestry of life's embrace,
We find our strength, our sacred space.

Heartfelt Topography

In valleys low and mountains high,
Feelings rise and often sigh.
Each contour tells a tale untold,
As moments shift from warm to cold.

A landscape drawn of every dream,
Where hope is not a distant theme.
Paths of pain and joy combine,
Creating space where hearts align.

Through rivers deep and skies so wide,
Emotions flow like shifting tide.
With every bend, we learn and grow,
In the heart's map, love's river flows.

With rocky trails and gentle streams,
We navigate through tangled dreams.
In every hollow, light will gleam,
Reflecting all that we've believed.

So let us chart this land of soul,
With every heartbeat, make us whole.
In topography of the heart,
We find the truth, our brand new start.

Explorations of Empathetic Landscapes

In valleys where silence breathes light,
Hearts open wide, embracing the night.
Mountains echo whispers of trust,
Paths of compassion rise from the dust.

The rivers sing songs of deep care,
Flowing through spaces both tender and rare.
Fields of understanding bloom and expand,
Guiding lost souls with a gentle hand.

Amidst towering trees, we find our place,
Roots intertwining, a warm embrace.
With each step forward, we forge anew,
Landscapes of empathy, dreamers pursue.

In shadows of doubt, we find the light,
Mapping our journeys, hearts taking flight.
Exploring horizons, together we soar,
In every step, we nurture and more.

Emergent visions rise with the dawn,
In the heart of each life, hope is reborn.
Together we build a vibrant new home,
In empathetic landscapes, we wander and roam.

The Language of Listening

In the stillness before the storm,
Words are quiet, emotions warm.
Listening deeply, hearts align,
Echoes of presence, pure and divine.

Voices like rivers share what they bear,
Stories of longing echo in the air.
With each word spoken, bridges arise,
Understanding blooms under open skies.

The art of listening, a language anew,
In silence we gather, in stillness we grew.
Every heartbeat whispers tales untold,
As wisdom unfolds, a treasure to hold.

Eyes meet in truth, compassion ignites,
Conversations unfurl like stars on nights.
Within the connections, we find our ground,
In the language of listening, love is found.

Between every pause, there's magic and grace,
Crafting a cosmos we all can embrace.
So let us listen, let silence flow,
In the language of listening, our spirits grow.

Merging Voyages

On waves of wonder, we set our course,
Navigating dreams with unyielding force.
Two hearts adrift in a vast open sea,
Charting the waters of what could be.

With sails of hope and winds of intent,
Every moment shared, a story well-spent.
The horizon beckons with mysteries near,
Merging our journeys, erasing the fear.

In the dance of the tides, we find our way,
Blossoming cultures in vivid display.
As colors collide, we create a new song,
Together we flourish, where we both belong.

Anchors of kindness hold us in place,
In the currents of life, we find our grace.
Mapping our travels, weaving our hopes,
Merging voyages, discovering new scopes.

Through storms that may come, we weather the fight,
Trusting each other to guide through the night.
With each gentle wave, our spirits entwine,
Merging our journeys, our lives intertwine.

The Bridge Beyond Boundaries

Where rivers of difference flow deep and wide,
We build a bridge where love can reside.
Crafted from hope, and the dreams we share,
A path to each other, a life beyond care.

In the heart of the storm, we find our strength,
The bridge stretches far, spanning great lengths.
Each step taken, a story we weave,
Connected by faith, in which we believe.

Through valleys of doubt, we travel as one,
Holding each other till battles are won.
With courage and grace, we traverse the night,
On bridges of unity, we seek the light.

As horizons expand, new visions arise,
Guiding our hearts towards blue-painted skies.
Where boundaries fade and kindness prevails,
On the bridge of compassion, each love never fails.

Together we rise, like a phoenix takes flight,
Embracing the challenges, ready to fight.
A bridge without limits, where dreams intertwine,
In the bridge beyond boundaries, our spirits shine.

Pathways of Connection

Along the winding trail we walk,
Sharing thoughts and silent talk.
Footprints left in gentle grace,
In every smile, a warm embrace.

Beneath the stars, we search and find,
The threads that weave our hearts entwined.
Every turn, a story near,
In laughter's echo, we draw near.

Through shadows deep and colors bright,
We light the path, dispel the night.
With open hearts, we bridge the space,
Creating bonds that time can't chase.

In fleeting moments, love's refrain,
We rise above our fear and pain.
Each pathway leads to further dreams,
Connected souls, or so it seems.

Together we roam, though worlds apart,
Finding solace in the heart.
Hand in hand, we'll face the dawn,
On pathways shared, we journey on.

Cartography of Compassion

On the map of hearts we trace,
Lines of kindness, every place.
With each gesture drawn in light,
Love's geography in our sight.

Mountains high, valleys low,
Every human story flows.
In the compass of our souls,
Finding warmth that makes us whole.

Through the storms and quiet days,
Compassion's light will guide our ways.
With every tear, a river streams,
Navigating shared dreams.

Markers stand in joy and pain,
Reminders of what we can gain.
As we travel, hearts align,
In this cartography, we find.

With every step, we build anew,
Compassion's map will guide us through.
Together we will draw the lines,
Creating spaces where love shines.

Navigating the Heart

In the waters of emotion deep,
We navigate the dreams we keep.
With sails of hope and winds of grace,
Finding solace in every space.

Charting courses near and far,
Listening close to every star.
In the tides of laughter and tears,
Our hearts will guide us through the years.

With gentle whispers, we will steer,
Through storms and sunsets drawing near.
In unison, our spirits soar,
Navigating love forevermore.

Anchor down in moments still,
With every beat, a steadfast will.
Together we sail, against the tide,
In the heart's vast ocean, we abide.

Through uncharted waters, we will roam,
Finding peace, creating home.
With every heartbeat, we explore,
Navigating love, forevermore.

Uncharted Conversations

In whispers soft, our words take flight,
Exploring depths, igniting light.
With every question, seeking truth,
Uncharted paths reclaim our youth.

Through laughter shared and silence too,
Every moment, a chance to view.
With hearts open wide, we dive,
Into the stories that come alive.

We venture forth on winding trails,
With honest tones that break the veils.
In vulnerability, we grow,
Exploring realms we thought we'd know.

With courage found in every breath,
In connection strong, we conquer death.
Through conversations, bonds are made,
Uncharted waters, unafraid.

So let us speak our truths sincere,
In every heartbeat, love draws near.
In uncharted realms, we unite,
Conversations spark, igniting light.

Navigating Heartstrings

In the quiet night, whispers call,
Faint echoes of love, we feel them all.
Like soft winds through trees, they sway,
Binding our souls in a gentle play.

With every step, we find our way,
Across the shadows, where dreams lay.
Hearts entwined, as stories unfold,
In vibrant hues, our lives are told.

Moments shared, a tapestry we weave,
Among the stars, we dare to believe.
Through laughter and tears, we build our trust,
In every heartbeat, it's more than just.

Through tides of change, our spirits roam,
Searching for warmth, a place called home.
Hand in hand, through storms we stand,
Navigating life, a shared command.

United we shine, through dark and light,
Guiding each other, through every fight.
In harmony's dance, we never stray,
Navigating heartstrings, come what may.

Paths of Connection

Winding trails through the forest green,
Moments of joy, where souls convene.
Each step forward, we leave a trace,
In paths of connection, we find our place.

Whispers of kindness, gently spread,
In the warm embrace, where fears are shed.
With open hearts, we learn to see,
Each other's journeys, wild and free.

Through laughter's echo, we gather near,
Shadows dissolve when love is clear.
Together we forge, unyielding ties,
Beneath the vast and open skies.

In every glance, worlds collide,
Awakening spirits we cannot hide.
The bonds we forge will ever endure,
In paths of connection, we are secure.

As seasons change, we still remain,
Walking together through joy and pain.
Hand in hand, through life's design,
Paths of connection, forever entwined.

Threads of Empathy

In the fabric of life, we stitch with care,
Threads of empathy, binding us there.
With every heartbeat, we start to learn,
The fire of kindness, we continually burn.

Through struggles shared, we find our strength,
In every moment, we grow in length.
Sewn with compassion, our stories entwined,
Threads of empathy, intricately designed.

When voices tremble, and shadows loom,
We stand together, dispelling the gloom.
With every shared tear, we weave anew,
In the tapestry of life, the colors break through.

Unraveling layers, we seek to feel,
In every connection, hearts start to heal.
With gentle hands, we mend what's torn,
Threads of empathy, forever reborn.

So as we journey through life's grand quilt,
We cherish the love, woven and built.
In unity's shine, we rise above,
Threads of empathy, stitched with love.

Bridges Across the Divide

In the distance stands a bridge of grace,
Connecting hearts in this vast space.
With every word, we span the gap,
Bridges across the divide, we map.

In gentle whispers, the silence breaks,
Finding common ground, as the earth shakes.
With listening ear, we build each inch,
Bridges to hope, where hearts can clinch.

When walls rise high, we choose to climb,
Brick by brick, in heartfelt rhyme.
Each gesture shared, a steadfast guide,
Offering light, where darkness tried.

Together we stand, as one and whole,
Forging connections, healing the soul.
With every step, we strengthen the tie,
Bridges across the divide, we try.

So let us gather, hand in hand,
Across the bridge, where futures stand.
In unity's echo, we challenge the tide,
Bridges across the divide, our hearts abide.

A Symphony of Voices

In the hush of evening light,
Whispers soar on wings of night.
Songs of hope dance in the air,
Each note a dream we gladly share.

Echoes blend in harmony,
Telling tales of you and me.
Together, we create a sound,
In unity, our hearts are bound.

From valleys deep to mountains high,
Voices rise, reaching the sky.
A tapestry of every tone,
In this symphony, we're not alone.

Through laughter, tears, and gentle cries,
Our spirit weaves, it never lies.
In every heartbeat, every sigh,
Together we'll forever fly.

So let us sing from dusk till dawn,
A melody that keeps us warm.
In every voice, a light bestowed,
Together, we have found our road.

Aligning Our Selves

In quiet moments of the day,
We seek the truth along the way.
To find our center, hearts unite,
In clarity, we find our light.

With every breath, we draw in peace,
From worries, we find our release.
In stillness, we begin to see,
The beauty in our harmony.

As stars align in velvet skies,
We recognize our silent cries.
In each connection, we stand tall,
Together we can face it all.

The journey's path may twist and turn,
But lessons learned will help us learn.
With open hearts and minds so clear,
We walk the way, free from fear.

So let us gather, side by side,
With courage ample as our guide.
In unity, our spirits thrive,
Together, we will come alive.

The Discovery Expedition

In shadows deep, we wander far,
With hopes alight like distant stars.
The world unfolds with every step,
Adventure calls, in dreams, we leapt.

Through rustling leaves and rivers wide,
We find the thrill that lives inside.
With every turn, new wonders bloom,
In unknown paths, we dispel gloom.

Maps uncharted guide our way,
To hidden gems where spirits play.
With open minds, we chase the thrill,
Exploring depths, we climb each hill.

As voices blend in nature's choir,
We kindle dreams that never tire.
In every heartbeat, each embrace,
We dance upon this timeless space.

So let the journey take its course,
With hearts as one, we feel the force.
Together we become the quest,
In every challenge, we are blessed.

Embracing Each Footstep

With every tread upon this ground,
We carve our path, our stories found.
In every heartbeat, moments pass,
Embracing life, we let joy amass.

The echoes of the past remind,
Of lessons learned, of ties that bind.
As feet align on trails so true,
We find our strength, we start anew.

In sunlit days and starry nights,
We gather dreams, igniting lights.
With every stumble, every stride,
In shared adventures, we confide.

So laugh and love with open hearts,
As each experience imparts.
In every moment, let us see,
The beauty in our unity.

Together facing winds of change,
In each footstep, we rearrange.
With hope and kindness as our guide,
We journey on, forever side by side.

Treasures of Truth

In the quiet of the night,
Whispers share their light.
Secrets held so tight,
Glisten like stars in flight.

Beneath the surface deep,
Lies the wisdom we keep.
In silence, we reap,
The treasures that don't sleep.

In laughter and in tears,
We unravel our fears.
Through love, we steer,
The truths that bring us near.

Fragments of a heart,
Crafted like fine art.
With each note, we chart,
A journey from the start.

So let us seek and find,
A bond that intertwines.
In the depths, we bind,
The treasures we've outlined.

Weaving a Tapestry of Dialogue

Threads of thought entwined,
In colors well-defined.
Voices blend and bind,
Creating pathways aligned.

Each story holds a place,
In this shared embrace.
With kindness, we trace,
The tapestry we face.

Echoes of our dreams,
Flow like silent streams.
Crafting complex themes,
Together, so it seems.

With every word we say,
We pave a brighter way.
In the dance of play,
Connection's here to stay.

So let us weave with grace,
In this sacred space.
A tapestry we chase,
Of dialogue we embrace.

Echoes of Authenticity

In the shadows speaks truth,
A voice that calls in youth.
Genuine and uncouth,
It carries the heart's proof.

Moments that we share,
In honesty, we dare.
With each breath of air,
Authentic light laid bare.

Unfolding in the now,
We let go of the how.
With a solemn vow,
To live this way, we bow.

Ripples form as we trust,
Our words, a sacred gust.
In the bonds robust,
We find what's truly just.

For echoes fill the room,
In the light, dispel gloom.
With hearts in full bloom,
Authenticity's our tune.

Currents of Cooperation

In the river of our minds,
A current ties and binds.
Together, it unwinds,
Strength in all mankind.

Hands reaching through the flow,
Where the seeds of hope grow.
In sharing, we know,
The power we bestow.

Through valleys and through peaks,
In harmony, we speak.
From the strong to the meek,
The future that we seek.

With courage on the rise,
We see through each other's eyes.
In unity, the prize,
As one, our spirits fly.

So let us chart the course,
With hearts as a source.
In currents, we endorse,
Cooperation's sure force.

Exploring the Space Between

In silent whispers, we drift apart,
Finding solace in the unseen art.
A thread of hope in shadows cast,
Exploring moments, memories vast.

Echoes linger in the void,
A delicate dance, our hearts deployed.
In the stillness, we seek to find,
The fragile line that binds the mind.

Stars above, they guide the way,
Through uncharted paths where dreams play.
With every breath, we navigate,
The space between, our hearts create.

Connections woven, thread by thread,
In the silence, our souls are fed.
Together we rise, together we fall,
In the space between, we find it all.

So let us wander, hand in hand,
In this vast, unclaimed land.
For in each heartbeat, we conceive,
The beauty of what we believe.

The Tapestry of Togetherness

In vibrant hues, our lives entwine,
A tapestry rich, with stories fine.
Threads of laughter, woven tight,
In the warmth of shared delight.

Each moment stitched with care and love,
Like whispers carried by the dove.
We paint our dreams with joy and grace,
In the heart's quiet, sacred space.

Fingers meet in gentle clasp,
Holding memories in a warm grasp.
Through trials faced, we stand as one,
In the depth of night, we greet the sun.

Together we rise, like dawn's embrace,
In unity's strength, we find our place.
A patchwork quilt, a shared refrain,
The tapestry of joy, woven from pain.

In every stitch, a story told,
Of warmth and strength, of hearts bold.
Together we weave, through thick and thin,
In this tapestry, love will always win.

In Search of True North

Across the landscapes, we roam wide,
Seeking the truth that doth abide.
With stars as our compass, we chart the skies,
In the quest for wisdom that never dies.

Through valleys low and mountains steep,
In shadows deep, our dreams we keep.
With every step, we seek to learn,
As the fires of passion brightly burn.

The maps of old guide our ways,
Yet new horizons beg our gaze.
In every heart, a burning flame,
In search of purpose, we play the game.

Winds of change whisper soft and low,
As we uncover paths to grow.
In the depths of night, we find our light,
Guiding us through the endless fight.

Together we journey, hand in hand,
In the search for truth, we take a stand.
For every heartbeat fuels our quest,
In search of true north, we find our rest.

Portraits of Perception

In the gallery of life's embrace,
We capture moments, time and space.
Portraits painted with colors bright,
Each brushstroke tells of joy and plight.

Through different lenses, we see the world,
In a vibrant swirl, our fates unfurled.
Each reflection holds a story dear,
A testament to love, hope, and fear.

We frame the laughter, the tears, the pain,
In vibrant hues, like sun and rain.
A canvas wide, a tale to share,
Of every heart that dares to care.

In fleeting glances, we find our truth,
In the wisdom gathered from our youth.
Every portrait holds a piece of soul,
In this life's gallery, we are whole.

So let us cherish each masterpiece,
As the brush of time creates our peace.
In every portrait, a tale unfolds,
The beauty of perception, forever told.

Milton Keynes UK
Ingram Content Group UK Ltd.
UKHW021954151124
451186UK00007B/243